LOUIS ARMSTRONG: A JAZZ MASTER

For Bb Instruments

MW00682535

CONTENTS

BUTTER AND EGG MAN 6
COME BACK SWEET PAPA 8
CORNET CHOP SUEY 3
GULLY LOW BLUES 10
GUT BUCKET BLUES 12
HEEBIE JEEBIES 48
HOTTER THAN THAT 14
I'M NOT ROUGH 16
IRISH BLACK BOTTOM 26
JAZZ LIPS 18
KNEE DROPS 20
MUGGLES 22
MY MONDAY DATE 24
ORIENTAL STRUT 29
POTATO HEAD BLUES 34
SKIT-DAT-DE-DAT 32
STRUTTIN' WITH SOME BARBECUE 37
SUNSET CAFE STOMP 42
TIGHT LIKE THIS 40
TWO DEUCES 45

Edited by RONNY SCHIFF
Graphics by LEN FREAS

LOUIS ARMSTRONG

There have been fifty golden years of Louis Armstrong's music, and it still hasn't aged. This folio contains twenty of Louis Armstrong's most interesting solos transcribed originally by jazzman Lee Castle. They are clean, uncomplicated solos that are fine examples of basic jazz lines.

Louis Armstrong began his career in the early '20's with King Oliver and then with Fletcher Henderson. He formed his own group in 1925 with Earl Hines. In the late '20's, he became the headliner with big bands and exploded into prominence. The '30's took Louis to Europe where American jazz was getting wide acclaim. By mid-30's, he was playing regular radio broadcasts beamed from major clubs like the Cotton Club and the Grand Terrace, and had appeared in several motion pictures.

After World War II Louis switched from big bands to a more informal sextet and stayed with that type of musical format the rest of his life. He became the international spokesman for traditional American jazz. He covered Africa for the U.S. State Department. He also toured an incredible amount of countries all over the world, including Hungary, where he played for a crowd of 93,000 in Budapest's football stadium.

Satchmo in his 60's surprised a world in its 60's by recording a hit ("Hello Dolly") that outsold most of the major rock tunes on the charts.

In every biography on Satchmo, there is a comment on the basic simplicity and beauty of his form of jazz. In the original print of this folio, Frank Driggs stated: "With the passing years, jazz has increased in complexity, the result of the use of more complicated harmonies; therefore, the nature of the improvised line has become highly intricate......... The lesson to be learned from Louis Armstrong (and from all great jazz improvisers) is that essentially once the technical problems are overcome, the essence of jazz is in the feeling expressed. Therefore, even if a person's interest lies in shaping a style based on more contemporary jazzman, one should spend some time with these uncomplicated solos."

At the end of each solo there are notes to trumpet players relating to alternative fingerings for producing certain notes. However, for sax and clarinet players, as well as trumpet players, catching these tunes on recordings will assist one in being able to reproduce them. All the tunes in this book are on Columbia's album "The Louis Armstrong Story."

CORNET CHOP SUEY

By LOUIS ARMSTRONG

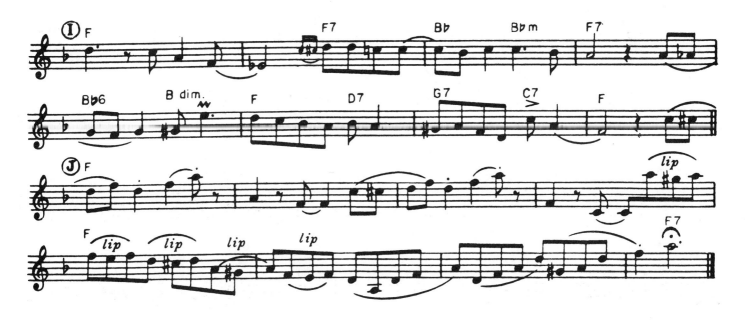

CORNET CHOP SUEY

Louis starts this one with a four bar "intro" that is typical of the style that brought him fame. One nice feature about it is its simplicity, making it easy for duplication by most players. Accent the first note in the group of eighth notes as indicated.

The break two bars before [C] is also typically Louis.

In [F] the piano strikes just the first note in each bar and Louis takes successive breaks for sixteen bars. The trumpet student can get a great deal of good studying and memorizing these bars. All sixteen bars can be used as part of a "hot" chorus in numbers where the chord sequence is similar. With slight changes the entirety (16 bars) may be used in many jazz solos.

The two bars before [G] form a good pattern and can be used often.

Beginning at the end of the fourth bar of [J], take note of the "lip" markings. This is played by using the fingering of the first note of each grouping for all the subsequent notes marked with a "lip". The middle note (the lowest one) is brought out by slackening the lip muscles, thereby lowering the pitch.

Beginning on the last half of the sixth bar of [J], normal fingering must be resumed.

This solo is perhaps the greatest of all Armstrong originals and contains a wealth of material for those interested in learning how to play Louis' style.

BUTTER AND EGG MAN

By LOUIS ARMSTRONG
and PERCY VENABLE

BUTTER AND EGG MAN

Butter and Egg Man is a real neat and clean solo, typically Louis, at ease, playing so lyrically that you almost hear a singer perform in an easy, unhurried fashion with lots of meaning. Not too many tricks.

The one different effect is the figure at end of (D) showing the tone and false fingering of the [musical figure] which, when played makes a good sound.

*Watch All Markings.

COME BACK SWEET PAPA

By PAUL BARBARIN and
LUIS C. RUSSELL

COME BACK SWEET PAPA

In Come Back Sweet Papa, the shake, staccato notes and rhythmical figures, familiar in other solos, are being utilized to make and build a solo of good playing and nice listening. This is one of Louis' real good ones.

Watch All Markings.

GULLY LOW BLUES

By LOUIS ARMSTRONG

GULLY LOW BLUES

This one starts with a lot of spark (M. M. at 208) and slows up at the break at [B] to Blues Tempo. (M. M. 112)

Beginning at [C] Louis employs the shake (⌢). This can be done in two ways. 1. If one normally uses a hand vibrato, a shake is effected by greatly exaggerating the vibrato. Move the trumpet just as one would do in producing a hand vibrato, but quite violently, in order to bring the next upper interval (with no change in fingering) into play. It should sound like a fast trill. 2. If one normally uses a lip (or jaw) vibrato, a shake may be produced by exaggerating the jaw movement.

GUT BUCKET BLUES

By LOUIS ARMSTRONG

GUT BUCKET BLUES

Gut Bucket Blues is a fine study of different versions of 12 bar blues. Here Louis plays from the heart with a real low-down feeling staying in low register in order to send his message. Note all markings. If not done, the player will lose all effectivenesss.

*Watch All Markings.

HOTTER THAN THAT

By LILLIAN HARDIN ARMSTRONG

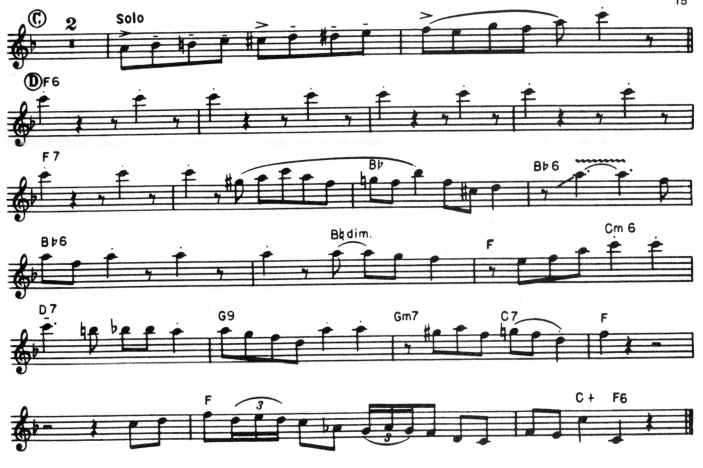

HOTTER THAN THAT

The first 4 bars of [A] are typically Louis. Many of our present-day trumpeters fit these four bars (exactly as they are, note for note) into whatever hot chorus they happen to play, and usually employ it at the beginning of a chorus just as Armstrong does at [A].

The chorus he plays from [A] to [C] is an excellent one with a good solid "beat" all the way.

I'M NOT ROUGH

By LILLIAN HARDIN ARMSTRONG

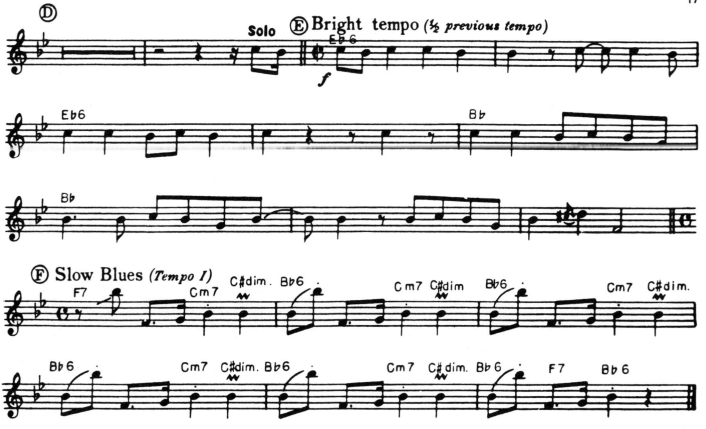

I'M NOT ROUGH

Louis begins at [A] by playing the Blues as only he can play it. Any good trumpeter can play the notes but it is mainly the "feel" and his tone that give the "drive".

Of course, the rhythms he uses are wonderfully effective and especially so when he "lips" certain notes (6th bar of A, 6th bar of [B] and 10 & 11 of [C], this last one more prolonged than the former two.)

JAZZ LIPS

By LILLIAN HARDIN ARMSTRONG

JAZZ LIPS

A "growl" (usually represented by GR above the note or phrase) is produced by vibrating the vocal chords in the throat. To acquire it, hum (as in singing) and at the same time, place the trumpet on the lips. Play a phrase (preferably in the middle or low register) while continuing to hum. A slight soreness of the throat might be noticed but with a little practice, it will disappear, and growling in all registers becomes quite feasible.

A smooth, even hum (wide vibrations) will produce a rough growl. However, either type should be used with good taste at all times, depending on the mood of the number.

The basic difference between a growl and flutter (FL) is that the growl is played as described above, while the flutter is produced by vibrating the tongue against the roof of the mouth, as when one rolls the "R" in everyday speech.

KNEE DROPS

By LILLIAN HARDIN ARMSTRONG

KNEE DROPS

Knee Drops is another easy going solo, going at a bright clip, with many of Louis' old and famous little phrases heard on many of his record solos, especially (A). At (D), he begins to build up and up to (break) before (E) and finally going strong till the very end.

*Watch All Markings.

MUGGLES

By LOUIS ARMSTRONG

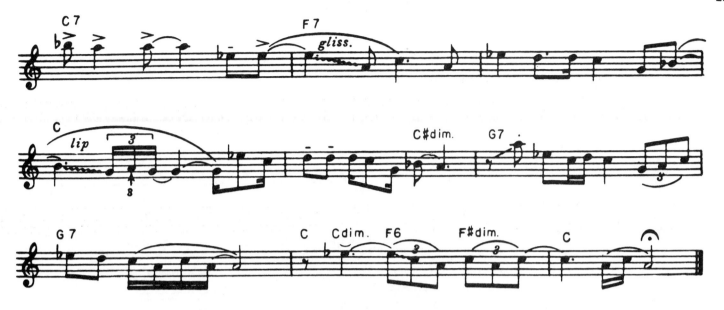

MUGGLES

Terminology

- ·   A dot over any given note indicates sharp tongueing.

- ⌇   Indicates a fast vibrato.

- \>   Indicates an accent.

- ⌣   Indicates a "bend" where the player changes the pitch without changing the fingering.

  Example: (notation) EQUALS (notation) *Legit. Version*

- ⌁   Indicates a "shake" or fast trill.

- —   Indicates soft tongueing where the note should be given full value.

- *lip* (notation)   Indicates a glissando from the upper to the lower note. This is produced by relaxing the lip from the upper note and dropping the pitch as far as possible. The lower note is then approached by "half-valving" into it.

- *gliss* (notation)   Indicates a use of "half-valving" plus lip slur from low to high.

- *gliss* (notation)   Indicates a use of "half-valving" plus relaxed lip pressure from high to low.

- (notation)   Indicates a "rough rip" up to the note.

- (notation)   Indicates a "fall off" produced by "half-valving" and a sudden lessening of lip tension.

It is extremely important to evaluate properly the use of vibrato as it pertains to the numbers in this book. To get a good "feel" in the sound of this jazz, a fast vibrato is imperative — not a "nanny" but a fast, even fluctuation of pitch. It should be emphasized that Armstrong almost always plays with a fast, close vibrato, especially at the end of phrases. This makes for Louis' special "feel" and "drive".

MY MONDAY DATE

By EARL HINES

25

MY MONDAY DATE

Two bars before [C] should be played straight eighth notes (Louis' style).

The chorus from [C] to [E] is exceptionally good. Louis plays a number of rhythms here of the type he will always be remembered for.

Note the terrific "break" at bars 1 & 2 or [F]. For this to be effective, accent the first note of each set of two eighth notes, and observe the crescendo right up to the last note.

IRISH BLACK BOTTOM

By LOUIS ARMSTRONG
and PERCY VENABLE

27

28

IRISH BLACK BOTTOM

Irish Black Bottom is a very good composition for study, without too many flourishings. It has very good continuity instead. This proves that some solos can be good and effective without too many tricks. Markings are needed in many cases. That's why they are there. This solo was good without them. There are a few — heed them.

*Watch All Markings.

ORIENTAL STRUT

By JOHN A. ST. CYR

ORIENTAL STRUT

In Oriental Strut, we have, indeed, a strut, in a melody, oriental in feeling but with a good beat.

At letter (C) a good effect is made by 1 bar breaks for 24 bars before going on full till (F) where it begins to go back to simpler figure, after which it rides to the end. Very different.

*Watch All Markings.

SKIT-DAT-DE-DAT

By LILLIAN HARDIN ARMSTRONG

SKIT-DAT-DE-DAT

Skit-Dat-De-Dat is a very good and interesting study of 6-8-10 bar phrases of contrasts with 2 bar fill-ins by pianist, in between, for player to take breath before each new and good attack. This solo starts by long whole notes, with a gradual change to rhythmical patterns which delight player and listener.

Watch All Markings.

POTATO HEAD BLUES

By LOUIS ARMSTRONG

STRUTTIN' WITH SOME BARBECUE

By LILLIAN HARDIN ARMSTRONG

38

STRUTTIN' WITH SOME BARBECUE

The four bar break that Louis plays at the beginning of [C] is another original pattern that is still being used by leading trumpeters — in all keys.

The four groups of triplets two bars before section [D] will be most effectively played if the first note of each set is strongly accented. Also note the accents in bars 9 & 10 of [D]. The lower notes of each group of three are relatively unimportant and should be played softly. Produce the feeling of throwing them away while you accent the first note of each group by tonguing hard.

TIGHT LIKE THIS

By A. CURL

TIGHT LIKE THIS

From letter [D] on, Louis plays some very difficult "double time" rhythm in a virtuoso style and with his individual touch. In spite of the fact that Louis uses a lot of techniques in his jazz choruses, he still retains the essential "beat".

This is one of his great contributions to the field of jazz trumpet.

SUNSET CAFE STOMP

By LOUIS ARMSTRONG
and PERCY VENABLE

SUNSET CAFE STOMP

Sunset Cafe Stomp is a solo which will surely make the player think as well as play. He will have to divide carefully and at the same time, watch the accents. Lots of playing with very little rest. Relief comes along at (F) with a piano solo for 3 bars.

At (G) there is again a constant build-up with little rest, but very interesting to the very end.

*Watch All Markings.

TWO DEUCES

By LILLIAN HARDIN ARMSTRONG

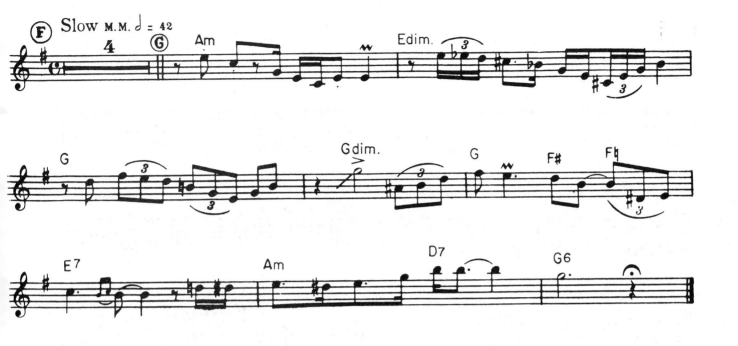

TWO DEUCES

In Two Deuces, we find a fine example of original thought and feeling, embracing two different styles and tempos, (slow blues and fast tempo). In the slow blues movement, we find lots of lip slurrings and shakes, plus 16th note phrases which double up the rhythm. At (E), there is a change of pace to faster tempo, till at (F) we go back to the slow and easy tempo in which this very good solo began.

*Watch All Markings.

HEEBIE JEEBIES

By BOYD ATKINS